MW01593214

DREAM
BIG
Dream! C. Sam Read

Patches

VISITS THE JUNGLE

C. Sam Read

Patches
Visits the Jungle
by C. Sam Read
Illustrations by NorViance Henry

Printed in the United States of America

ISBN 9781498408431

www.xulonpress.com

DEDICATION
For Jeffrey...my dude!

Future works of Dr. Kotina W. Hall will be penned as C. Sam Read. C. Sam Read was created in part to inspire children to read and as a dedication to her late uncle, Sam Russaw, who always brought humor to "The Compound."

Today I am feeling sad. Mom just announced that Charlie Mae won't be visiting today because she didn't clean her room.

Mom says I'll survive without
Charlie Mae for one day.
She even suggested
I play with Jackson.
"Impossible!"
Nothing could
be worse!

I spoke too soon;
it begins to rain.
This has to be
the worst day ever!

Jackson knocks on my door to ask
if I would like to play. "Of course not!
Your games are boring, and you don't know
how to play the fun games Charlie Mae and I like.
I will sit here and wait for the rain to stop."

"Have it your way. I will be in my room
exploring Jungle Town," said Jackson.

"No such place!"' thought Patches.

As Patches sat on her bed looking out the window, she could hear strange sounds coming from Jackson's room. She heard roars and screeches. It sounded very much like a jungle in there. It even sounded like Jackson was having fun.

Patches couldn't believe she was actually thinking about playing with Jackson. The more she watched the rain fall, the more she realized that playing with Jackson was the only way to make the time go by faster.

Patches knocked on Jackson's door, but there was no answer. She called his name, but Jackson still didn't answer. She slowly cracked the door to see what was going on.

JACKSON

What do you know? Jackson's room had transformed into an amazing animal kingdom. There were monkeys, lions and birds everywhere. Tall trees and flowers were there, too.

Patches yelled louder for Jackson, and finally he answered. "I am down below getting food for the animals. Grab the flashlight and follow my voice."

Patches grabbed the flashlight and waited for Jackson to yell again. Sure enough, Jackson yelled, and Patches was on her way. Patches heard another scream, but it wasn't Jackson. "Watch out for the lizards. If you step on one, more will come. Walk quietly but swiftly," the voice yelled.

When *Patches* arrived, she saw Jackson picking berries and bananas with a little girl. "We were expecting you, Fitz. We thought you would never arrive," said Jackson.

"Impossible!" exclaimed *Patches*. "How did you create this?"

"Create what?" asked Jackson.

"This – this jungle!" *Patches* yelled.

"You mean Jungle Town?" asked Jackson. "Mom always said we can use our imagination to create anything we want."

"So...welcome to Jungle Town. We are delighted to have you. I am your leader, Jungle Jackson."

"What are you going to do with all these berries and bananas?" asked *Patches*.

"We are going to feed the animals before we depart for the island. Night is almost upon us. We don't want to get caught in the jungle at night," said Jungle Jackson.

"Yes, we better get going," said the girl.

"By the way, who is this girl?" asked *Patches*.

"Oh, her name is Mary," said Jungle Jackson.

"Mary?" inquired *Patches*.

"Yes, Mary," Jungle Jackson quickly remarked.

Patches and Mary followed as Jungle Jackson led the way
back through the thick jungle. Jackson said, "Be careful
ladies, and remember to keep moving. Watch your step
and keep your eyes on your leader."

"Leader!" shouted *Patches*. "Hmm. I don't know about that."

"My story. My lead," exclaimed Jungle Jackson. "And keep your voice down so you don't awaken the creepy, crawling critters," whispered Jungle Jackson.

The animals were waiting for Jungle Jackson because he knew exactly what each animal liked. Patches and Mary assisted, too. Once all the animals were fed, Jungle Jackson turned to Mary and *Patches* to inform them that it was time to depart.

As soon as they entered the boat, they heard a knock on the door. It was Mom announcing that the rain had stopped. Jungle Jackson, Mary and *Patches* cheered.

"Don't forget to put your toys away," yelled Mom.

"We won't!" *Patches* responded.

"Are you going to help us, Mary?" asked Patches.
"Unfortunately, I cannot. I must be going now," said Mary.

Jungle Jackson turned to Mary and said, "Well, I guess we will see you next time."

"It was nice to meet you Mary," said Patches.

"The pleasure was indeed mine," stated Mary.

Mary leaped from the boat and plunged into the deep water. Her shiny fin lit up the night sky.

"Well, what do you know? Mary is a mermaid!" shouted Patches.

"Yes, she is!" Jungle Jackson happily said.

"Thank you for letting me visit Jungle Town with you," stated Patches.

"Not a problem at all," said Jungle Jackson.

Jackson flipped on the lights and began to put away his toys.

"What happened to Jungle Town?" asked Patches.

Jackson said, "Just like the toys, I had to put Jungle Town away."

"Where did you put it?" Patches asked.

"Oh, I tucked it away in my mind," responded Jackson.

"You tucked Jungle Town away in your mind? Impossible! How did you do that?" Patches questioned.

"It was really easy," said Jackson. "I just closed my eyes and placed Jungle Town by the photo shop at the mall next to the place where we love to get ice cream."

"Oh, I like the location!" giggled Patches.

"I do have one final question though. Of all of the names in the world, why did you name the mermaid, Mary?" Patches curiously asked.

Jackson quickly replied, "Mom always says, 'Whenever you want to have lots of fun, the more the Mary-er!'"

They both laughed and headed outside.

Brothers don't always get it right, but boy are they funny when they try!

CPSIA information can be obtained
at www.ICGtesting.com
Printed in the USA
BVHW012020230620
581835BV00004B/14